AMERICAN NEEDLEWORK 1776/1976

AMERICAN NEEDLEWORK
1776/1976 Leslie Tillett

Needlepoint and Crewel Patterns Adapted from Historic American Images

Foreword by Rose Kennedy

New York Graphic Society, Boston

Diagrams by Roberta Frauwirth
Photographs by Edward Grazda
Designed by Margaret Dodd

Composed in 11 on 14 Helvetica by DEKR Corporation, Woburn, Massachusetts
Printed by Meehan-Tooker, East Rutherford, New Jersey
Bound by A. Horowitz and Son, Fairfield, New Jersey

Library of Congress Cataloging in Publication Data

Tillett, Leslie, 1915-
   American needlework, 1776-1976.

   1. Needlework--Patterns. 2. Needlework, American.
3. Crewelwork--Patterns. I. Title.
TT753.T54   746.4'4   75-9096
ISBN 0-8212-0664-8

First Edition

Printed in the United States of America

FOREWORD

This is the right time for a book on bicentennial needlework. Not only is the 200th anniversary near, but the interest in needlework by all sorts of Americans is widespread and growing.

Of course one doesn't have to do needlework to like it or collect it. I don't actually use needle and yarn myself, but in the years of putting together homes for my family I've managed to accumulate a fair number of samplers along with American furniture, and one particularly cherished piece of needlepoint, a piano bench cover now in Hyannisport, was made by my mother.

Those three basic tools, the needle, the plow, and the trowel, have been with us for a long time. Though most of us can't get back to the plow or the trowel, the needle seems to be attracting more and more Americans as we approach 1976.

It is a curious fact to me that at eighty-five I have been here for over forty per cent of this country's young life. I say "young" because as nations live, two hundred years means youth. Compared to our ancient mother country of Britain, we here are still making our first grade samplers.

The British immigrants brought over the tradition of needlework; the making of samplers was general before the first revolution and survived the second, or industrial, revolution. Since then the succeeding waves of immigration from all lands have enriched our needlework heritage. Needlework began to disappear after the third revolution, or Civil War, but now it is coming back strongly during what often seems like a fourth revolution of great equalizing changes.

Leslie Tillett has been designing for many years and in many fields, so it is not surprising to see him interested in needlework. This ability to make the new out of the old is his specialty. It is fascinating to see how the original source of inspiration can be adapted to our times and skills yet retain the original flavor in a kind of recycling process. Maybe the whole nation is going through a kind of recycling and will come out better than ever.

I like the American Rose pattern, and of course I'm pleased that it is dedicated to me. I am also particularly interested in the adaptation of Martha Washington's little known needlepoint which Leslie Tillett and his wife discovered at Rosedown in Louisiana.

The design inspired by the Molley Russell 1776 sampler in the Smithsonian, with three different kinds of stitch treatments, should prove interesting to everyone and seems to demonstrate that the more things change, the more they remain the same . . . .

The early Chinese tea label from the Museum of the American China Trade in Milton, Massachusetts, has lent itself to a very interesting pattern, and the design of the Boston Tea Party adapted from an old French toile is amusing.

Since Betsy Ross used her needle, Americans have sewn, embroidered, and needleworked. It is wonderful to see how all kinds of people—old, young, black, white, men and women—have turned to this rewarding experience. The book includes design ideas for older people and for men and for children. My own grandchildren have made slippers and other small things in needlepoint.

When Jacqueline Kennedy Onassis asked me if I would care to write this foreword, she reminded me that Leslie Tillett and his wife were the people she asked to start The Design Works of Bedford-Stuyvesant in the Bedford-Stuyvesant restoration project founded by Robert Kennedy. Perhaps it is not too much to hope that this book will be a much smaller but similar inspiration in the growing world of needlework, helping to stitch up the old wounds of time.

ROSE F. KENNEDY

August 2, 1974

PREFACE

For several years I have been doing research on the Bicentennial for product design, and some time ago I began to notice how many historic American images lent themselves to needlework. The idea of doing a book crystallized in 1970, when my wife and I discovered a piece of needlepoint by Martha Washington at Rosedown Plantation in Louisiana.

My interest in needlework really dates from work with the Nantucket Needlery. There I worked out a new palette for the dyed yarns and pioneered the screen printing of canvas for needlework kits. Like most people who become involved with needlework, I was soon hooked, and since then I have been designing needlework kits and finished needlework. I also added needlework to the activities of The Design Works of Bedford-Stuyvesant, a craft project I started in the black ghetto of Brooklyn at the request of Jacqueline Onassis. When I mentioned the forthcoming book to her, she suggested that Rose Kennedy would be interested in it because of her Americana collection.

The average worker today is not only cut off from the land but is suffering from unemployed hands. But our hands have been making things for hundreds of thousands of years and they can't just stop without making us unhappy. The recent surge in interest in needlework is the first positive and widespread indication of a return to handwork, a return which I believe is going to spread still more widely. Automation will mean still more "time on our hands," and clever hands—and all hands are clever to some degree—must be worked.

It will be seen from the contents of the book that I have no objection to translating one technique to another—I see nothing sacrilegious in using a stenciled chair as the basis for a needlework pattern. Nor do I think there is any virtue in being "authentic" in the sense of reproducing an old pattern literally. I try to see those old images with new eyes, and it is in this recycling that some creative ingenuity enters.

A large number of people have helped bring this book into being, among them the makers of the original models we photographed: Nob and Non Utsumi, Barbara Christopher, Beatrice Malkin, Bernice Barsky, Frank Kitchen, Lynn Riker, Rosa May Winston, Barbara Lowenstein, Louise Fili, Girard Goodenough, Ralph Cherry. Particularly helpful was Mr. Kitchen's fine rendering of the Shaker Tree and the "Do Not Tread On Me" banner.

Lastly I want to extend my thanks to Mrs. Joseph P. Kennedy for taking an interest in the book and writing her charming Foreword, and to Jacqueline Kennedy Onassis for suggesting it to her.

L. T.

ON COLOR: A DESIGNER'S APPROACH

The color chart on page 10 is based on a selection of Paternayan's Persian yarn #W 45 A, which comes in 316 colors. The chart is printed well, but you are still looking at printer's ink rather than dyed wool, so the actual yarns should be seen before you make any final decisions about color. The names are my own, with some historical overtones rubbing off from the book and from my studies of dyestuff history. (See Notes on Color Names.)

I started professional life as a color chemist, mixing colors in the family textile plant in Amersham, Buckinghamshire, in England—a job I was saved from by the war. I have always found this technical color background useful, and admit to strong feelings on the subject of synthetic dyes.

There is a kind of mythology of "natural" colors—many people think vegetable colors are always better than the "harsh, bright," synthetic dyes. They forget that most vegetable dyes are very fugitive, so that what they see now in old fabrics is quite faded from the original hues. They ignore the fact that by diluting or gray-shading the anilines any variety of soft or pastel tones can be produced, in colors that are far more resistant to sun and water.

As to the criticism that synthetic dyes are less "natural" than vegetable dyes, I can only say that this is snobbism. After all, what is more natural than a lump of coal (the source of most anilines)? I'm reminded of "plastic" snobs who attack the material but ignore the form, forgetting their love of glass, one of the first malleable—plastic—materials.

Still, there is a romantic aura to vegetable dyes and some practical basis for the growing interest in them, because many of the sources—like goldenrod—can be grown or bought domestically. The old ingredients can still be found in imported indigo, madder, brazilwood, camwood, gum lac, fustic, barberry, chrome, sassafras, and persian berries. Even the fabled royal purple, from seashells, can be imported from Mexico, and there are a few weaver-dyers left in Mexico who use cochineal. I visited a sarape-weaver near Oaxaca who raised his own sheep for wool that his family spun into yarn. He had planted fields of the nopal cactus, which the cochineal bug lives on, and made red dyes from cochineal and all other colors from natural sources except for emerald green, which he admitted came from "Casa Dupon" (DuPont).

The color schemes illustrated may not always be to the taste of the needleworker or fit into a particular setting. I suggest they be treated with the utmost irreverence. But in replanning the color schemes, here are a few pointers to keep in mind:

Rule No. 1.: Nothing's sacred. Skies do not have to be blue or leaves green. The important thing in a design is the color *scheme*.

To get a preview, cut off bits of yarn in the colors you're planning, varying the amounts cut according to the relative amounts of each color in the overall design. For example, if a design calls for a few small leaves in one color, some big flat flowers in another color, and lot of solid-color background, you should try to duplicate these color proportions. Arrange the yarns in some sort of flat shape to see if the colors look compatible to your eye.

When you begin the needlework, fill in the biggest areas first (except the background), because this will help you see how the combination is working. With a coated paper color chart (such as Color-Aid, available in most art supply shops) you can shuffle the color cards into new combinations, then cut pieces of paper and place them over the pattern motifs to see the effect.

The currently fashionable schemes are: red-pink-orange; browns with violets; and (always) black and white. But there are also white-on-white (various shades of white, cream, ivory, and so on), and black-on-black. When in doubt, you can always choose a monotone scheme, which need not be monotonous. The Willow Plate scheme, all blues and greens, is a useful one. Beware of the red monotone, though—it usually looks too sanguinary. Try accenting the monotones—a bit of yellow with the blues, for example, or a touch of pink with all greens. I'm currently using an Ivy-Plaster scheme, which combines several leaf greens with various whites. And I still like the classic neutral scheme of light brown, beige, taupe, and grays.

Goußes de l'Anil   *Anil*

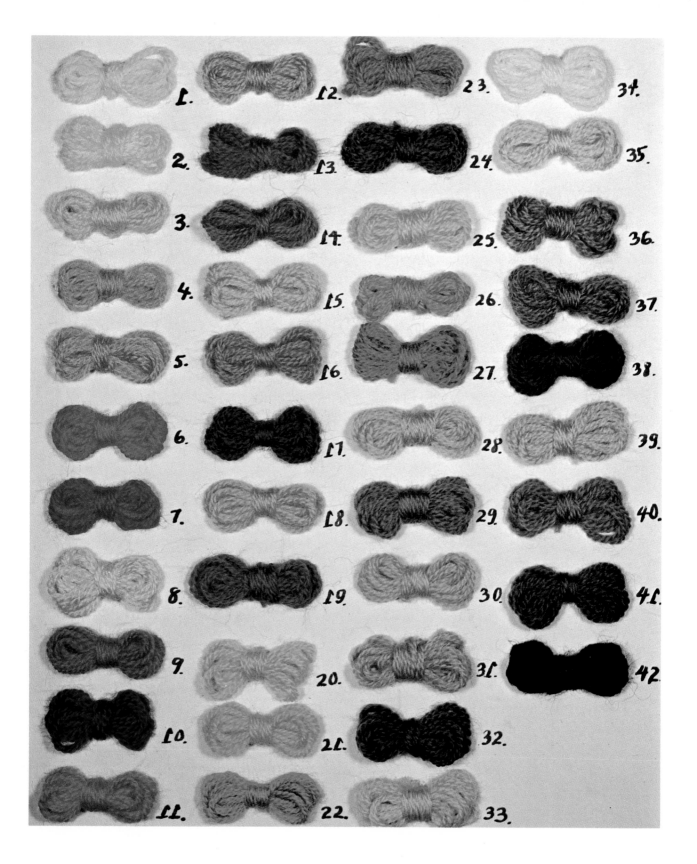

COLOR CHART

Our Numbers and Names of Colors	Paternayan Persian Numbers		Our Numbers and Names of Colors	Paternayan Persian Numbers
1 Citron	456		22 Turquoise	728
2 Goldenrod	Y44		23 Hessian Blue	755
3 Saffron	Y40		24 Indigo	310
4 Marigold	965		25 Foam Green	589
5 Carrot	978		26 Grass Green	569
6 Bittersweet	958		27 Malachite	559
7 Redcoat	R10		28 Moss Green	570
8 Hydrangea Pink	831		29 Olive	510
9 Raspberry	232		30 Willow Green	550
10 Mulled Claret	236		31 Sage	590
11 Beetroot	827		32 Cedar	507
12 Roseash	294		33 Chartreuse Yellow	446
13 Cinnamon	414		34 Bleached White	
14 Woodrose	283		35 Parchment	153
15 Orchid	660		36 Linsey-woolsey	025
16 Crocus	650		37 Jute	134
17 Pansy	640		38 Beaver	113
18 Powdered Blue	743		39 Silver Dollar	186
19 Porcelain Blue	723		40 Gunmetal	182
20 Opal Blue	765		41 Charcoal	180
21 Hummingbird	748		42 Bark Black	050

Notes on Color Names

2 The color I call "Goldenrod" actually comes from the goldenrod plant. It is picked at the beginning of bloom time, dried, and boiled into the yarn with alum as a mordant.

7 My name "Redcoat" comes from the British soldiers' uniforms, which were made of wool of yarn dyed with madder, a plant whose cultivation Dolly Madison encouraged in this country. It was probably first imported from France by Thomas Jefferson.

10 "Mulled Claret"—a drink of the American gentry in Colonial times. It was made of claret wine, heated, usually with a hot poker.

18 The name "Powdered Blue" (now called "powder blue") comes from China, where workers blew powered cobalt onto porcelain before glazing it to a soft blue finish.

23 "Hessian Blue" derives not from the color of the Hessian mercenaries' uniforms (they wore British red), but from the duchy of Hesse, where the vegetable source of the color was grown. ("Prussian Blue" also came from that part of Germany.)

24 "Indigo," the main cash crop in the South before cotton took first place, was first raised in South Carolina in 1739 through the efforts of Eliza Pinckney. She obtained the plants from her father, the Governor of Antigua.

28 "Moss Green" is named for common moss, from which the yellowish substance is extracted that forms the color base.

36 "Linsey-woolsey" was a common fabric of Colonial times, a mixture of linen and wool often left unbleached, in its natural oatmeal-like color.

Alternative Color Schemes

With all this in mind I have listed below some basic alternative schemes that can be used in almost all the designs. Bear in mind that a color scheme depends for its effect on the *relative amounts of color used.* Therefore amounts appropriate for each scheme are shown graphically.

1. MIXED PASTELS

1	Citron	
8	Hydrangea Pink	
15	Orchid	
18	Powdered Blue	
20	Opal Blue	
25	Sea Green	

35 Parchment and/or 39 Silver Dollar could be used as ground or mixed in.

2. FIERCE RED

4	Marigold	
11	Beetroot	
6	Bittersweet	
7	Redcoat	

You could add 5 Carrot, 8 Hydrangea Pink, and 9 Raspberry, but in small areas. To change the background, use 12 Roseash or 39 Silver Dollar.

3. THE BLUE-GREEN DREAM

22	Hummingbird	
16	Crocus	
26	Grass Green	
27	Malachite	
19	Porcelain Blue	
18	Powered Blue	

4. OPPOSING NEUTRALS

12	Roseash	
38	Beaver	
37	Jute	
36	Linsey-woolsey	
40	Gunmetal	

You could use 13 Cinnamon as accent; 38 Beaver could be used as a dark contrast or as background. 14 Woodrose and 41 Charcoal could also be added.

5. PORTUGUESE TILE

1	Citron	
2	Goldenrod	
3	Saffron	
18	Powdered Blue	
19	Porcelain Blue	

23 Hessian Blue and 24 Indigo can also be added.

6. LEATHER AND AMETHYST

12	Roseash	
13	Cinnamon	
14	Woodrose	
15	Orchid	
16	Crocus	
17	Pansy	

7. IVY ON PLASTER

34	Bleached White	
25	Sea Green	
26	Grass Green	
27	Malachite	
29	Olive	
30	Willow Green	

8. TEMPERED STEEL

37	Jute	
40	Gunmetal	
41	Charcoal	
42	Bark Black	

THE PATTERNS

14

(Photograph Courtesy of the Smithsonian Institution, Washington, D.C.)

Alphabet Sampler

This is one of the most representative and attractive of the countless samplers sewn by American girls in the eighteenth and nineteenth centuries. Jemima Gorham, born August 28, 1773, worked the sampler at Mrs. Usher's School, Bristol, Connecticut, in 1790—the second year of Washington's presidency. She was already seventeen, for the obligatory sampler work was not confined to little girls.

   The needlepoint adaptation is a considerably simplified version of Jemima's detailed original. The numbers and lower-case letters are omitted, as well as the following poem:

> Let spotless innocence and truth
>   My every action guide
> And guard my inexperienced youth
>   From vanity and pride.

The sampler is now in the Smithsonian Institution.

COLOR KEY

☑ 1 Purple
☒ 2 Lavender
☐ 3 Orange
☐ 4 Aqua
☒ Green
☑ Brown
☐ Cream (background)
☐ White

Alphabet Sampler

FINISHED SIZE:

12½" × 14"

MATERIALS:

14 mesh to the inch mono canvas. 3-ply Persian tapestry yarn in the colors specified in the color key.

DIRECTIONS:

Bind the edges of the canvas with masking tape to prevent raveling. Separate the strands of the 3-ply yarn; use two strands together to work the stitches. Work the design in the Diagonal Stitch, following the diagram and color key.

The diagram for the border is shown on pages 126–127.

17

General Waschingdon and His Ledy

This pattern is based on a freely drawn version of a Pennsylvania Dutch watercolor of the late eighteenth century, now in the Abby Aldrich Rockefeller Folk Art Collection at Williamsburg. The inscriptions, in true folk-art-style, read simply, "Exselenc Georg General Waschingdon" and "Ledy Waschingdon."

The Pennsylvania Dutch (not Dutch at all, but German, the misnomer arising from the spelling and the anglicized pronunciation of "Deutsch") are famous for the brightly colored and naively charming designs they applied to their objects of daily use—from their drinking glasses to their barns.

I have tried to retain the flavor of the original, with its stiff, almost rigid drawing and primitive detailing. This very stiffness lends itself to the angularity of needlepoint, where, regardless of expertise, the needleworker must follow the lines of the canvas.

COLOR KEY

⊠ 1   Dark Blue

2   Medium Blue

⊞ 3   Turquoise

◪ 4   Dark Brown

5   Mustard (background)

⊡ 6   Red

☑ 7   Orange

⊡ 8   Pink

⑤ 9   Gold

☐ 10   Tweed { 1 strand Olive Green / 1 strand Yellow

◪ 11   Tweed { 1 strand White / 1 strand Yellow

◼ 12   Black

☐ 13   White

General Waschingdon and His Ledy

FINISHED SIZE:

15½" × 19½"

MATERIALS:

14 mesh to the inch mono canvas. 3-ply Persian tapestry yarn in the colors indicated in the color key.

DIRECTIONS:

Bind the edges of the canvas with masking tape to prevent raveling. Separate the 3-ply yarn, using two strands together for the stitches. The tweeds are worked by combining one strand of each color indicated. Work needlepoint in the Diagonal Stitch, starting at the upper right corner. The upper row of the design is two repeats of the couple in the diagram, but for the figures in the center the man's arm overlaps the woman and his coat touches her skirt (see illustration). The lower row also shows two couples, but with the arms of the outer figures, rather than the central pair, overlapped. The entire design is centered within the area indicated by the finished size; the background color completes the design.

21

Martha Washington's Needlepoint

After Martha Washington was widowed in 1799, she lived in seclusion, rarely seeing anyone other than family and close friends. During this time she did a great deal of needlework, the contemporary equivalent of watching television. My wife and I discovered this piece at the Rosedown Plantation near St. Francisville, Louisiana, in 1970. It came to Rosedown through a lady of the Custis family—a descendant of Martha's by her first husband, Daniel Parke Custis.

Martha's needlepoint is now framed in a Victorian firescreen, but perhaps it was originally part of an earlier firescreen—a common and useful way of displaying needlework in Martha's own time. The present owner of Rosedown, Milton R. Underwood, has kindly permitted us to use the design.

23

COLOR KEY

- ◪ 1   Dark Green
- ◨ 2   Medium Green
- ⊟ 3   Light Green
- ⊡ 4   Mint
- ⊠ 5   Dark Blue
- ◨ 6   Medium Blue
-    7   Pale Blue
- ◩ 8   Sky Blue
- ◨ 9   Dark Gray
-    10   Medium Gray
- ◪ 11   Light Gray
- ◼ 12   Dark Brown
- ☑ 13   Medium Brown
- ◪ 14   Dark Taupe
- ☐ 15   Beige
- ⊞ 16   Dark Rose
- ⊠ 17   Hot Pink
-    18   Pale Pink
- ◨ 19   Yellow
-    20   Flesh
- ◩ 21   Purple
- ☑ 22   Lavender
- ⊡ 23   White

Martha Washington's Needlepoint

FINISHED SIZE:

17″ × 14″

MATERIALS:

14 mesh to the inch mono canvas. 3-ply Persian tapestry yarn in the colors and amounts specified in the color key.

DIRECTIONS:

Bind the edges of the canvas with masking tape to prevent raveling. Separate the strands of the 3-ply yarn, using two strands together for the stitches. Starting at the upper right corner, work the design using the Diagonal Stitch. Follow the diagram and color key.

The diagram opposite shows the upper right quarter; it is continued on pages 128–130.

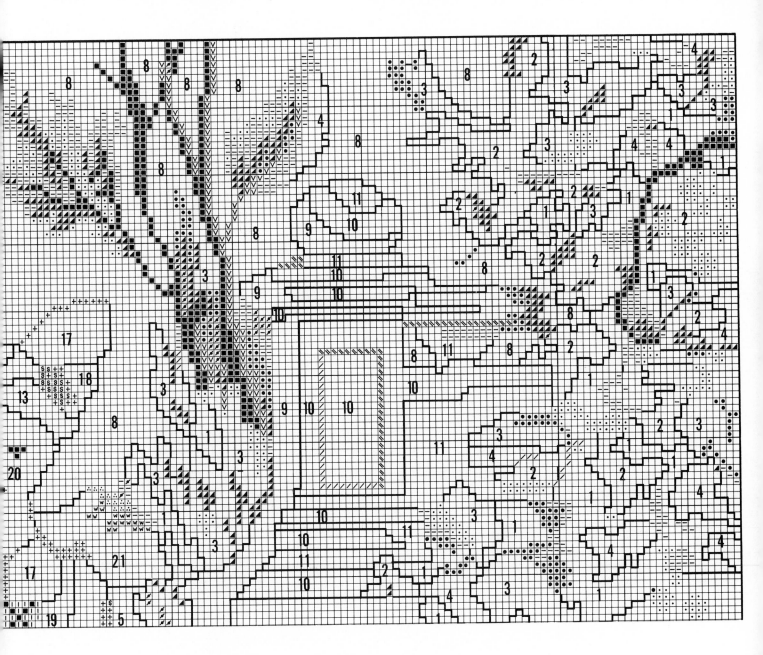

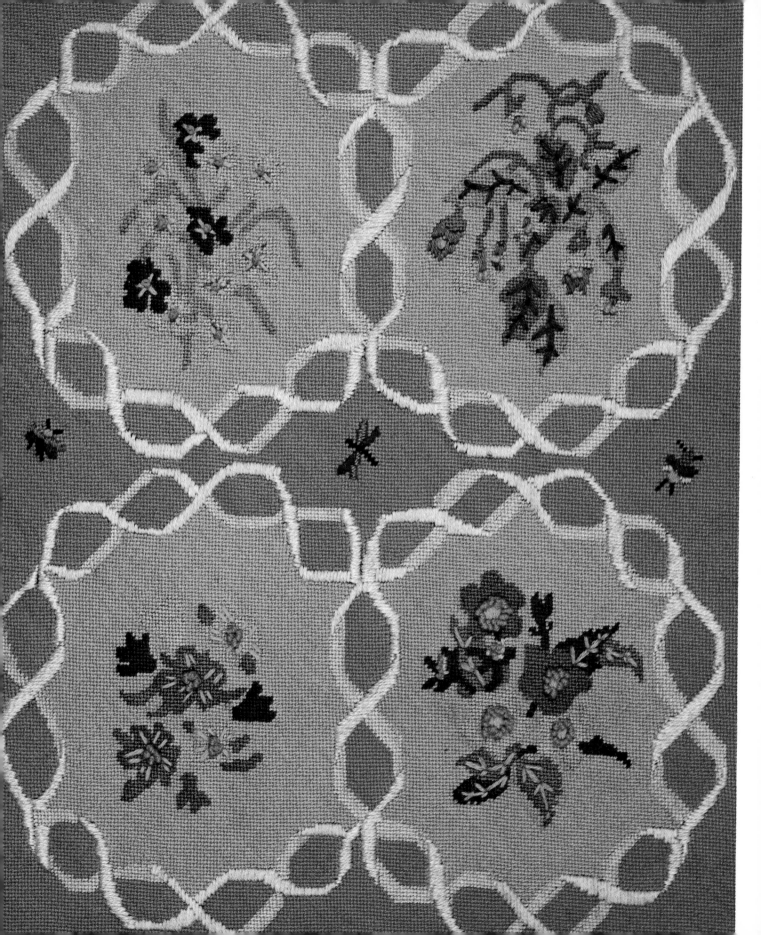

Martha Washington's Ballgown

In 1789 George Washington was inaugurated as President at Federal Hall in New York, the first capital of the United States. His wife Martha, however, remained at Mount Vernon, joining her husband in New York only when the presidential residence was ready.

This design is taken from a ballgown Martha wore at the levees (patterned after court receptions) she gave during her stay in New York. The low neckline is typical of fashionable dress in the late eighteenth century. Many of her other gowns were made from fabrics printed by John Hewson (see page 59).

The ballgown itself is now on a mannequin of Martha Washington in the Smithsonian Institution along with the gowns worn by all other former presidents' wives or hostesses at their respective inaugural balls.

Martha Washington's Ballgown

FINISHED SIZE:

20¼" × 16"

MATERIALS:

14 mesh to the inch mono canvas. 3-ply Persian tapestry yarn in the colors specified in the color key.

DIRECTIONS:

Bind the edges of the canvas with masking tape to prevent raveling. Separate the 3-ply yarn, using two of the strands together to work all areas of the design. Bargello stitches are indicated by heavy straight lines on the chart. Large dots on the chart are French Knots. The veins on the leaves are straight stitches worked over finished needlepoint areas. In the entwined borders, the Bargello is worked in white, and the needlepoint is worked in cream. All French Knots, the Bargello stitches within groups of French Knots, and straight accent lines on flowers are worked in gold.

Note: In order to reproduce the diagram at maximum size, it is shown at right angles to the color plate. The top of the diagram is the left side of the color plate.

COLOR KEY

- ☑ 1 Light Green
- ⊟ 2 Medium Green
- ◪ 3 Dark Green
- ⊠ 4 Brown
- ⊡ 5 Light Taupe
- 6 Dark Taupe
- 7 Medium Taupe
- 8 Dark Pink
- 9 Light Pink
- 10 Gold
- 11 Cream
- 12 White

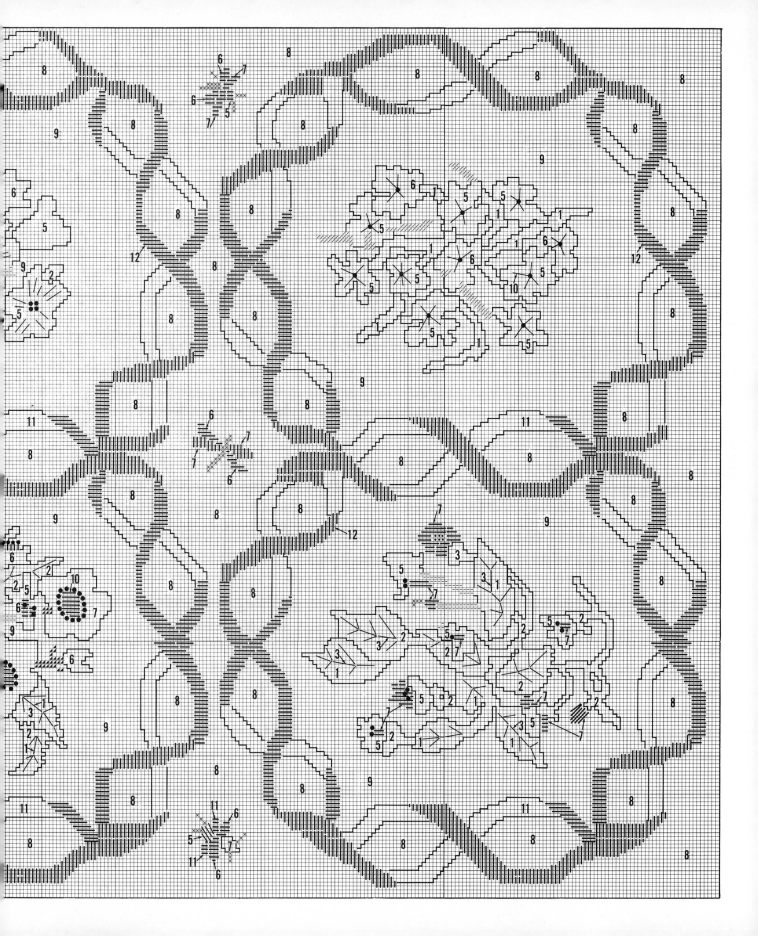

Bicentennial Medallion
1776-1976

The inspiration for this Bicentennial design was chiefly the many commemorative plaques made for the nation's Centennial celebration in 1876. I combined the best elements from thousands of eagles, laurel wreaths, and bunched stars that were used then.

The high point of the Centennial was the Great Philadelphia Exposition, where nations from all over the world were represented. Alexander Graham Bell's first demonstration of the telephone was one of the most memorable events of the Exposition.

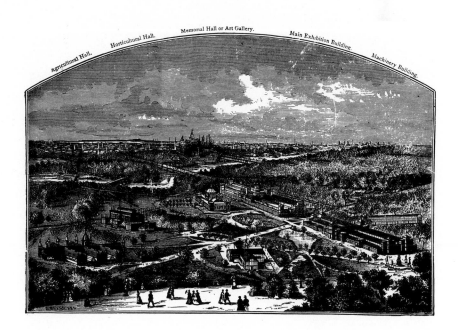

Bicentennial Medallion—1776-1976

FINISHED SIZE:

16″ diameter

MATERIALS:

14 mesh to the inch mono canvas. 3-ply Persian tapestry yarn in the colors specified in the color key. Transfer pencil or dressmaker's carbon.

DIRECTIONS:

Bind the edges of the canvas with masking tape to prevent raveling. Enlarge and transfer the design (see page 138). Separate the 3-ply yarn, using two strands together for the stitches. Work all areas of the design in the Basket Weave Bargello Stitch, following the color key.

Do Not Tread on Me

This design was inspired by the elegant banner of the United Company of the Train of Artillery, a regiment formed in Rhode Island in 1775. The whole banner is a more sophisticated version of the original forms shown here—even the contraction "don't" becomes the formal "do not."

The rattlesnake was a popular motif in Colonial times, signifying a force that gave due warning before it struck. It was a favorite image of Benjamin Franklin, who preferred the snake, shown in thirteen pieces, as the symbol of the thirteen colonies.

The two sketches on this page are the earliest versions of this rattlesnake motif. The "curled snake" flag designed by Christopher Gadsden is from 1775; the striped one, a naval flag also from 1775, was one of the first to bear the thirteen stripes.

1 Royal Blue
2 Medium Blue
3 Light Blue
4 Dark Teale
5 Light Teale
6 Pink
7 Rust
8 Black
9 Light Golden Brown
10 Tan
11 Brown
12 Dark Brown

Do Not Tread on Me

FINISHED SIZE:

17″ square

MATERIALS:

Gold-colored linen, 18″ square. 6-strand embroidery floss in colors specified in the color key. Transfer pencil or dressmaker's carbon.

DIRECTIONS:

Overcast the edges of the fabric or bind with masking tape to prevent raveling. Enlarge the design (see page 138), center over the linen, and transfer with either a transfer pencil or dressmaker's carbon.

Separate the 6-strand floss, using two strands together to work all embroidery. (Exception: use one strand only to work outlines of the letters and the dark brown lines in the snake's mouth.) Work Outline Stitch around all areas, in colors indicated, except stars. The stars, the background in the banners, ring and rope on anchor, cannon balls, the body, tail, mouth, and teeth of the snake, and small areas of cannon are done in Satin Stitch. The remainder is worked in close long and short straight stitches. All the lettering is white. The snake's teeth are white; its head and tail are rust; its body is in shades of brown, each shade worked for about 1″; refer to the illustration.

George Washington
Driving the Chariot of State

This splendid figure of George Washington driving a chariot drawn by twin leopards is a detail of a toile printed in England in 1782, as peace negotiations began (business was business even then). A similar toile printed by Oberkamp at Jouy in France was called "L'Indépendance Américaine." This example is from the Musée de Blérancourt, but many examples were brought to this country and are now in American museums.

The title of the English toile was "The Apotheosis of Benjamin Franklin and George Washington." Washington is shown driving the chariot of America (the seated figure), and the scene above shows Minerva guiding Franklin toward the Temple of Fame. The words on the banner, "Where Liberty Dwells, There is My Country," were used by Franklin. The shields at the bottom represent the three nations: the United States, symbolized by thirteen stars; France, by the sunburst; and Great Britain, by the Crosses of St. George and St. Andrew—all three countries finally at peace.

COLOR KEY

1 Gold
2 Blue
3 Red
4 Light Blue
5 Dark Green
6 Light Green
7 Rust
8 Brown
9 Dark Pink
10 Pink
11 Flesh
12 White
13 Black

George Washington
Driving the Chariot of State

FINISHED SIZE:

16½" × 17"

MATERIALS:

Heavyweight neutral-colored linen, 17½" × 18". 3-ply Persian yarn in the colors specified in the color key. Transfer pencil or dressmaker's carbon.

DIRECTIONS:

Overcast the edges of the fabric or bind with masking tape to prevent raveling. Enlarge the design (see page 138), center over the linen, and transfer with either a transfer pencil or dressmaker's carbon.

Separate the 3-ply yarn, using one strand for the stitches. All areas are worked in Satin Stitch except for the following: Facial features and stars are worked in short straight stitches. The flag, white lines on the banner, rims of chariot wheels and shield are worked in Outline Stitch in the colors indicated. The arms and head of the Indian and the leopards' heads are defined in Outline Stitch in black. Washington's buttons are French Knots. Refer to the illustration for the direction of Satin Stitches and also to check outlines.

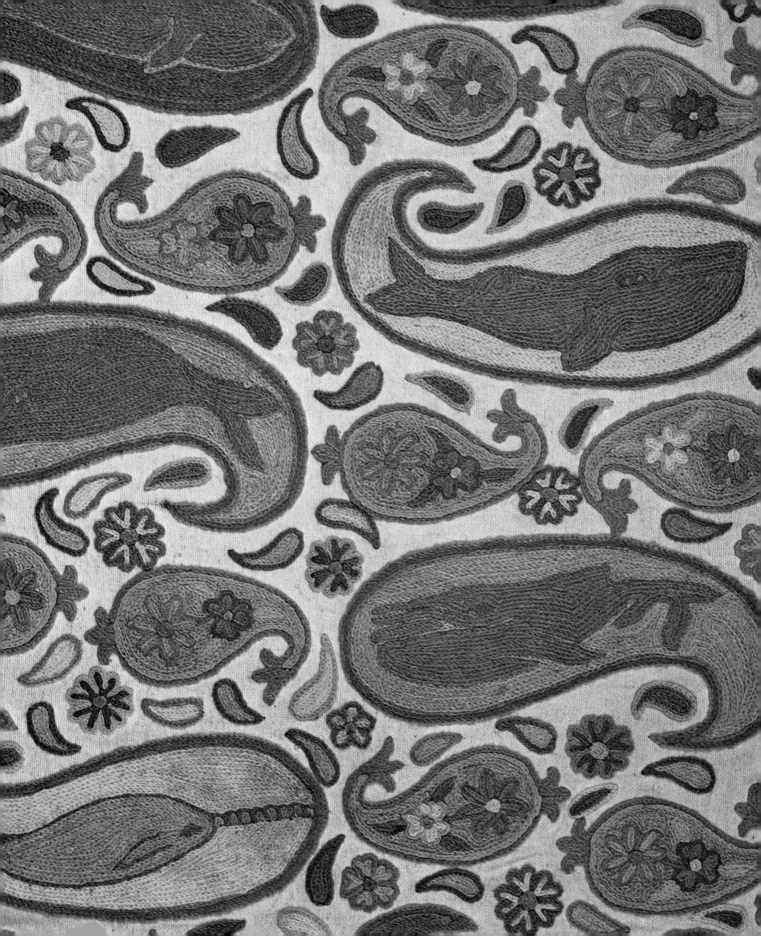

Whale Paisley

This design illustrates several of the different prey hunted by Nantucket whalers, including the humpback, the grampus, and the right whale—which was the most pursued. The whale with the long horn is the narwhal: its tusk was used for ivory. They are all set in the Indian, or Oriental, paisley motif, with a background of flowers and small paisleys.

The whale tooth shown above is worked in scrimshaw, a hobby popular with American seafarers in the nineteenth century. The similarity in the contours of the tooth, the bodies of the whales, and paisley patterns in general was the inspiration for the crewel design.

Whale Paisley

MATERIALS:

Hardanger cloth. 3-ply Persian tapestry yarn or crewel yarn in assorted pastel colors. Transfer pencil or dressmaker's carbon.

DIRECTIONS:

The design is a repeat of paisleys and flower motifs in three sizes. The finished size of the embroidery can be determined by the way you wish to use it—as a pillow or as a chair cover, for example. The diagram shows the motifs in their relative sizes. To make the pattern in the desired finished size, trace the repeat, inverting the large whale paisley each time; the medium-size paisleys alternately face and oppose each other; the small paisleys and flowers are placed at random. Refer to the illustration for the all-over pattern effect.

    Transfer the pattern to the fabric with transfer pencil or dressmaker's carbon. The whale paisleys are outlined in pink and blue, the floral paisleys in red-orange. The rest of the colors can be worked in pastel shades of your choice. Work the entire design in Chain Stitch, using crewel yarn or a single strand of 3-ply Persian yarn.

Benjamin Franklin Bouquet

About ten years ago I saw a fabric in the Museum of Printed Textiles in Mulhouse, France, that included a wonderful basket of flowers with bees and butterflies flitting around it. It was identified as coming from Oberkampf's printing plant at Jouy—which made the famous "toiles de Jouy"—in the late eighteenth century, and was displayed with fabrics exported to America. The pattern also incorporated the peace medal designed by Franklin, so I have named this delightful basket, which adapts well to needlepoint, for Ben Franklin. Incidentally, it was Franklin, always anxious to promote American business, who invited John Hewson (see the pattern on page 58) to come to America to establish his textile plant.

⊡1 White

◼ Dark Brown

☑2 Medium Brown

◩3 Tan

⊟4 Beige

◙5 Deep Red

⊞6 Hot Pink

☒ Deep Dusty Rose

⊡7 Pink

◪8 Gold

⊡9 Light Gold

◪10 Purple

⊟11 Lavender

◪ Dark Turquoise

◙ Turquoise

⊞12 Light Turquoise

◪13 Aqua

◪ Dark Green

◪14 Olive Green

◪ Light Olive Green

◪ Dark Blue-Green

◪ Medium Blue-Green

◪15 Light Blue-Green

◪ Pale Blue-Green

◪16 Rust

⊡17 Yellow

◻ Taupe (background)

Benjamin Franklin Bouquet

FINISHED SIZE:

17½″ × 18″

MATERIALS:

16 mesh to the inch Penelope canvas. 3-ply Persian tapestry yarn in the colors specified in the color key.

DIRECTIONS:

Bind the edges of the canvas with masking tape to prevent raveling. Separate the strands of the 3-ply yarn, using two strands together for the stitches. The diagram opposite shows the upper right quarter of the design; the lower left corner of this diagram should touch the center point of your canvas. Work the needlepoint in the Half-Cross-Stitch. Follow the diagram and color key. To complete, continue with the background color to the finished size.

48   The diagram is continued on pages 131–133.

Tea Chop

This charmingly rendered tea chest label is actually a "tea chop," or "facing." Originally a tea chop indicated that all the tea in a particular chest was from the same garden or plantation—its use was similar to markings on some wine bottles today. As the tea trade grew, the term "tea chop" took on a meaning akin to "brand," without reference to the origin of the tea.

   This tea chop, from the second half of the nineteenth century, is in a collection at the Museum of the American China Trade in Milton, Massachusetts. The collection of labels itself is well worth a visit, apart from the many other beautiful and unusual pieces exhibited in the museum.

Tea Chop

FINISHED SIZE:

11¾" × 12¼"

MATERIALS:

Hardanger cloth, ½ yard, ochre. 6-strand embroidery floss in red, gold, yellow, dark green, bright green, black, and white. Transfer pencil or dressmaker's carbon.

DIRECTIONS:

Separate the 6-strand floss and use three strands together for all embroidery. Enlarge the design (see page 138), center over fabric, and transfer. Following the diagram, outline all areas with short straight stitches, then fill in with cross-stitches. The lettering, branch, and figures are outlined with black. The large flowers in red and yellow are outlined in yellow. All leaves are bright green; stems are dark green. The small red flowers have white centers and black accent lines. The woman's dress is red with a green collar; the man is in green with a white cap and red ribbon. Their hands and faces, and the branch at their waists, are in gold Cross-Stitch. Refer to the diagram, color key, and illustration to complete the design.

54

Patchwork Quilt

Quilting was probably more highly developed in America than in any other country. It was not only a social group effort but also an early—and creative—recycling activity.

This round design is based on the traditional "Dresden Plate" quilt pattern, which was also known as the "Friendship Ring." For the pie-shaped pieces I have used printed-fabric designs in a selection that spans the first 150 years of American history. These include patterns by John Hewson, the most famous textile printer of the Revolutionary War period; Walters and Bedwell, the only printers to put their names on the fabric; and Archibald Rowan, whose business card read, "It used to be Archibald Rowan, Esquire, but now it is calicoe printer and dyer." Unfortunately, Rowan was forced out of business right after the Revolution by the British textile exporters, who still held a near-monopoly on the cloth trade despite their military defeat.

My sketch of the quilting bee on this page is a redrawing of an anonymous nineteenth-century painting.

Patchwork Quilt

FINISHED SIZE:

15½″ diameter

MATERIALS:

14 mesh to the inch mono canvas. 3-ply Persian tapestry yarn in the colors specified in the color key.

DIRECTIONS:

Bind the edges of the canvas with masking tape to prevent raveling. Separate the strands of the 3-ply yarn, using two strands together to work the stitches. Starting at the top of the diagram, work the design in Continental Stitch. Follow the diagram and color key. You may leave the center open, as shown in the illustration, for a wreath effect. Or, as indicated in the diagram, you may fill in the center with the Continental Stitch in sage green.

The diagram opposite shows the upper right quarter of the design; it is continued on pages 134–136.

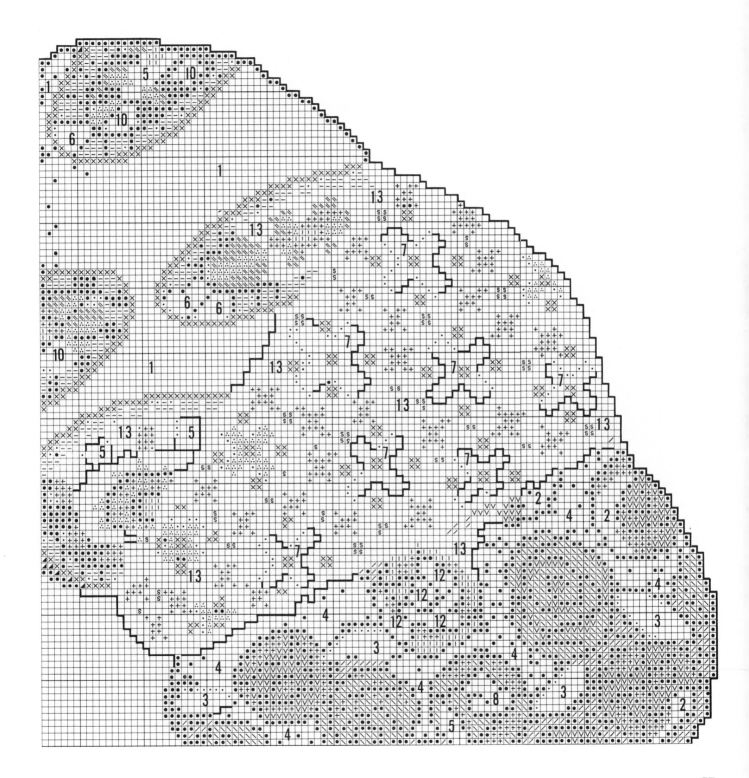

John Hewson Bouquet

John Hewson emigrated from England at the instigation of Benjamin Franklin shortly before the Revolutionary War and set up his own textile-printing plant in Philadelphia with equipment he had smuggled out of Britain. At that time the British government was fighting to maintain its lucrative monopoly on all fabrics going to the American colonies by prohibiting the export of textile machinery.

By 1774 Hewson was producing printed fabric, with his wife and children helping, and the following year Martha Washington commissioned him to design a kerchief for her. In 1776 he left his successful business to join the American Army as a captain. The British broke up his plant and captured him, but after the war Hewson rebuilt his plant and prospered. During celebrations of Pennsylvania's ratification of the Constitution on July 4, 1788, one of the floats drawn through the Philadelphia streets carried the Hewson family printing cloth.

The embroidery bouquet is adapted from a famous Hewson coverlet now in the Philadelphia Museum of Art.

(Reproduced at left, courtesy of the Philadelphia Museum of Art)

John Hewson Bouquet

FINISHED SIZE:

17″ × 17¼″

MATERIALS:

Heavyweight natural-colored linen, 18″ × 18¼″. 3-ply Persian yarn in the colors specified in the color key. Transfer pencil or dressmaker's carbon.

DIRECTIONS:

Overcast the edges of the fabric or bind with masking tape to prevent raveling. Enlarge the design (see page 138) and transfer to fabric. Separate the 3-ply yarn; use one strand for all embroidery. The stems are worked in Outline Stitch in colors indicated on color key; the cluster of stems tied together is worked in shades of green and brown. Use French Knots for dots on the diagram. The remainder of the embroidery is worked in Satin Stitch. Refer to diagram and illustration for color placement.

Confederate Flag

At least four flags were used by the South during the Civil War, but the most widely known today is the simple red field with blue Cross of Saint Andrew and thirteen white stars. This battle flag was suggested by General Pierre Gustave Toutant Beauregard of the Confederate Army, and it was used throughout the war.

In May 1863, the Confederate Congress officially adopted a flag with a white field bearing the battle emblem in the upper left corner. The predominantly white flag was frequently confused with a flag of surrender, however, so in 1865—just a few months before the end of the war—the Confederate Congress agreed to modify it. A red band was added at the right edge of the white field.

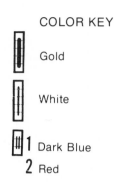
Confederate Flag

FINISHED SIZE:

14″ × 12″

MATERIALS:

14 mesh to the inch mono canvas. 3-ply Persian tapestry yarn in the colors indicated in the color key.

DIRECTIONS:

Bind the edges of the canvas with masking tape to prevent raveling. The diagram shows one-quarter of the entire design. The dotted line indicates the center rows, vertically and horizontally; do not repeat these rows when you enlarge the chart. To work the stars, white lines, and gold border, separate the three-ply yarn; use two strands together for the stitches. Areas marked for color 2 are worked in red in the Basket Weave Bargello Stitch, also using two strands. Areas marked for color 1 are worked in blue in the Bargello pattern indicated on the diagram, using all three strands of the yarn.

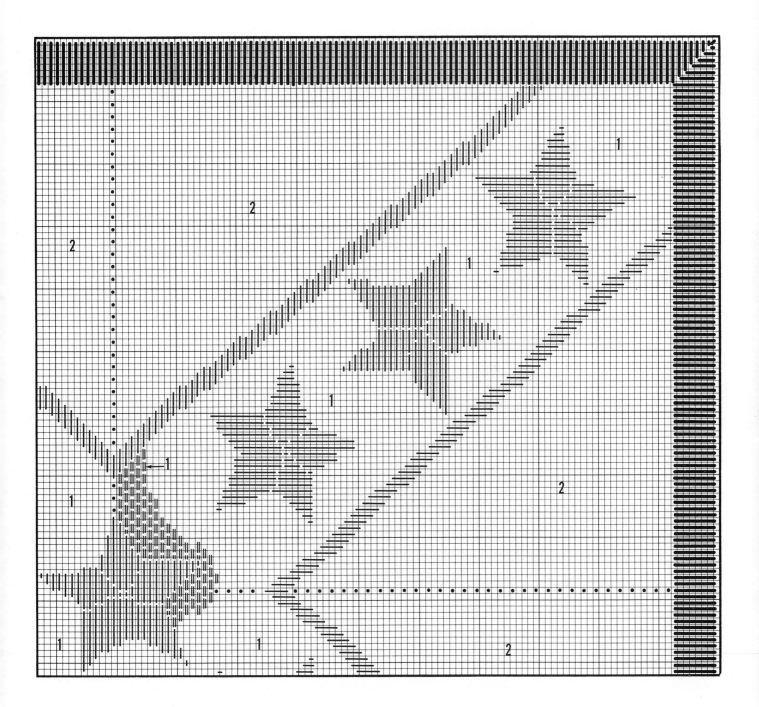

Crazy Horse and General Custer

Amos Bad Heart Buffalo, the great Sioux draftsman, drew the symbolic portrayal of the conflict between the Indians and the Whites that is the source of this pattern. The antagonists are represented by their two most famous leaders: General Custer is shown with the white man's weapon, the saber or "longknife," while Crazy Horse (Tasinke Witko) is shown with a primitive type of the stone club of his race. It is highly improbable that the artist (born in 1869) can ever have seen General Custer or Crazy Horse, who both died while he was still a small child. (The drawing is in the collection of H. B. Alexander.)

Custer, a vain man, was the only officer who ever fought in a velvet uniform. For the Battle of Little Big Horn, Custer—"Yellow Hair"—cut off his long hair and put it in his pocket so he wouldn't be recognized. The year of the Battle of Little Big Horn, 1876, was also the year of this country's Centennial. It marked one hundred years of freedom for America; for the Indian nation, it marked the last great stand for liberty. 67

Crazy Horse and General Custer

FINISHED SIZE:

13½″ × 11″

MATERIALS:

14 mesh to the inch mono canvas. 3-ply Persian tapestry yarn in colors indicated in the color key.

DIRECTIONS:

Bind the edges of the canvas with masking tape to prevent raveling. The diagram does not show all the plain area of the background; the principal motifs are centered horizontally and vertically. Separate the 3-ply yarn, using two strands together to work the design and background. The horses and riders are worked in the Continental Stitch in the colors indicated. The background is worked in Basket Weave Bargello; continue with this stitch until the canvas is covered to the desired finished size.

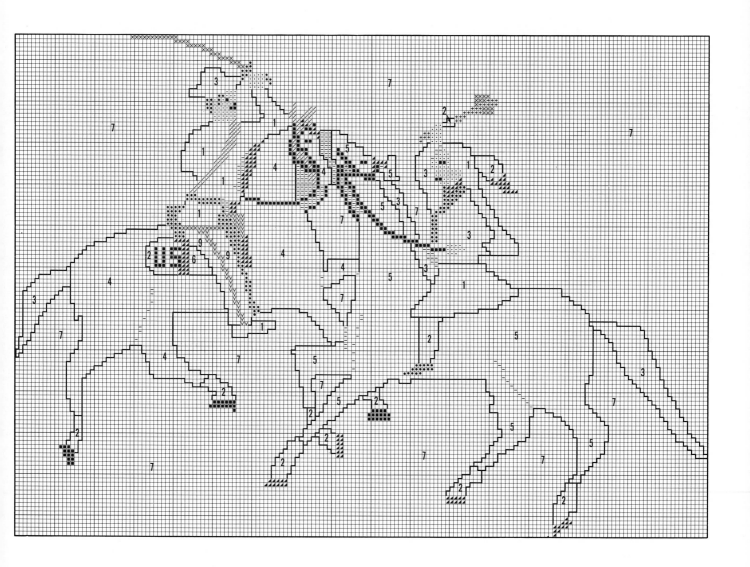

Heart Flag

This appealing heart-shaped flag by James Montgomery Flagg was one of four he produced during World War I. It appeared on the cover of *Leslie's Illustrated Weekly* of May 4, 1918, with the caption, "Is *your* heart right?"

James Montgomery Flagg was one of the most prominent American illustrators of the early part of this century. His posters, such as "Uncle Sam Wants You," are now collector's items.

COLOR KEY

1 Fuchsia
2 White
3 Blue

Heart Flag

FINISHED SIZE:

16½" × 17"

MATERIALS:

12 mesh to the inch mono canvas. 3-ply Persian yarn in colors specified in the color key.

DIRECTIONS:

Bind the edges of the canvas with masking tape to prevent raveling. The stars are worked in a simple Bargello Brick Stitch shown in the diagram. Work the rest of the design in Basket Weave Bargello, in the colors indicated in the diagram.

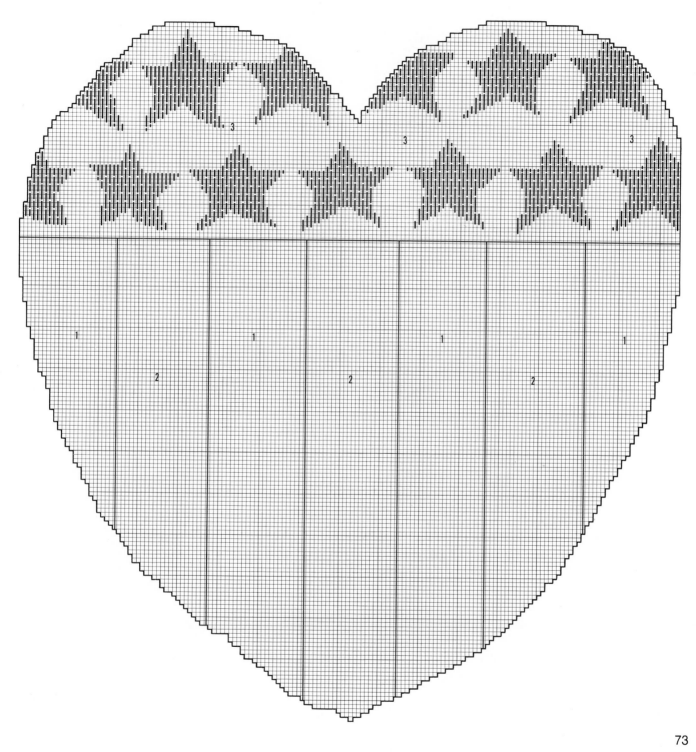

The Spirit of '76

This is yet another rendition from the famous painting by Archibald M. Willard, "The Spirit of '76"—which was actually made for the 1876 Centennial. It is based on the legend that tells of Americans facing defeat until a band of indomitable musicians marched into the front of the battle (what battle is not mentioned).

The image is also admirably suited to crewel work and would make a fine round pillow or picture.

The Spirit of '76

FINISHED SIZE:

14½″ diameter

MATERIALS:

12 mesh to the inch mono canvas. 3-ply Persian tapestry yarn in the colors indicated in the color key.

DIRECTIONS:

Bind the edges of the canvas with masking tape to prevent raveling. Separate the 3-ply yarn; use two strands together for the needlepoint. Beginning at the top right of the diagram, work the design in the Diagonal Stitch following the diagram and color key. The white stars in the flag are worked in Cross-Stitch. The buttons on the jacket of the flutist and on the cuffs of the small drummer are French Knots. Connect the gold needlepoint on the drums by running the strands of yarn underneath the stitches already worked. Using one strand of the black yarn, work a short stitch over one mesh of canvas, vertically or horizontally as indicated on the diagram, around the following areas to outline them: all white and flesh-color areas bordering on the background; the cuffs, headband, and flute of the flutist; the stockings and facial features of all three figures; the shirt and hair of the large drummer; and the drumsticks of the drummer boy. Refer to the illustration.

A detail of the pattern is shown in an enlarged diagram on page 137.

Stenciled Fruit

This design derives from the stenciled fruit patterns so popular on "fancy painted" chairs (and tole work too) in the second quarter of the nineteenth century. The patterns were stenciled in gilt, usually over black paint. The most famous examples of these chairs come from the factory of Lambert Hitchcock in Connecticut, where he pioneered assembly-line manufacture and was perhaps the first to produce a knocked-down (unassembled) chair.

Stenciled Fruit

FINISHED SIZE:

15″ square.

MATERIALS:

10 mesh to the inch mono or Penelope canvas. 3-ply Persian tapestry yarn in the colors specified in the color key.

DIRECTIONS:

Bind the edges of the canvas with masking tape to prevent raveling. Work the needlepoint in the Continental Stitch following the diagram and color key.

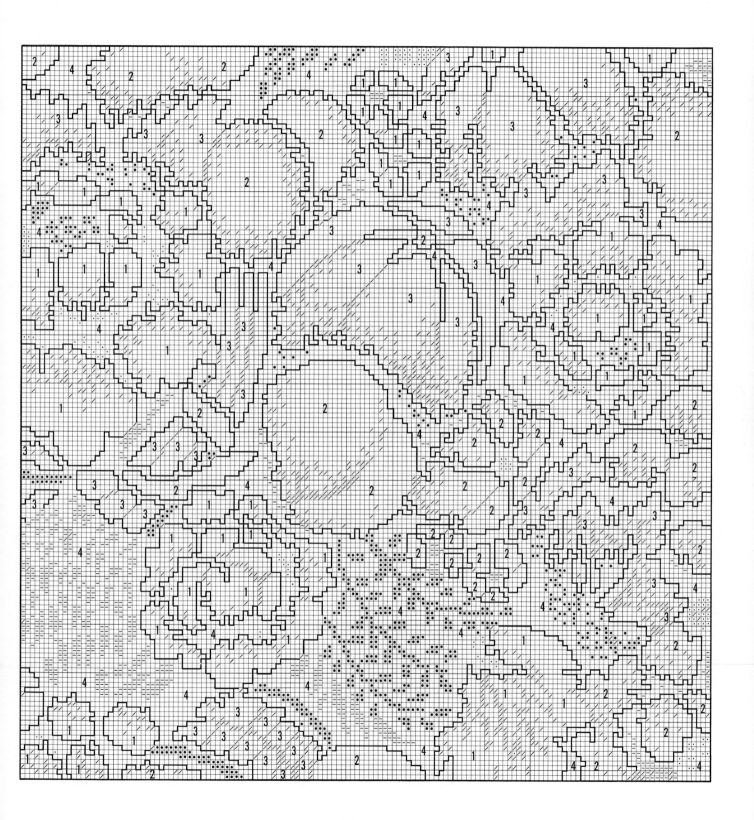

Shaker Tree of Life

This pattern is taken from an inspirational drawing done in ink and watercolor in 1854 by a Shaker named Hannah Cohoon, a member of the Hancock community. The original is now at the Shaker Community, Inc., Hancock, Massachusetts.

The Shakers, a religious, communal group, were properly known as the United Society of Believers in Christ's Second Appearing, but they were dubbed "Shakers" because of their dancing during religious services. The sect was founded in the 1760s by Ann Lee of Manchester, England, who came to this country with a small group of her followers in 1774. The sect made converts and prospered, but the Shakers adhered strictly to their doctrine of celibacy, and in 1974, their bicentennial year, they numbered only eleven souls.

Shaker Tree of Life

FINISHED SIZE:

14″ square

MATERIALS:

White linen, 15″ × 15″. 6-strand embroidery floss in the colors indicated in the color key. Transfer pencil or dressmaker's carbon.

DIRECTIONS:

Overcast the edges of the fabric to prevent raveling. Enlarge the design if desired (see page 138) and transfer to fabric. Separate the 6-strand floss and use three strands together to work the tree trunk and large branches in Satin Stitch. The smaller branches are worked with two strands of floss in Outline Stitch. Work all leaves lengthwise in Satin Stitch, using three strands of olive green. Then outline and criss-cross the Satin Stitches with one strand of brown, except where color 5, medium green, is indicated. The circles are filled with closely spaced French Knots, worked with three strands of floss in colors indicated. The area of grass and fallen leaves is worked in short straight stitches in a random pattern, using three strands of floss.

Washday

Clementine Hunter was born in 1882 on the Melrose Pecan Plantation, near Nachitotches in central Louisiana. There she worked as a fieldhand and house servant until 1946, when she began to paint.

Alberta Kinsey, a painter-guest at the plantation, left behind some brushes and paint, and Clementine began her first painting with these supplies, working on an old window shade. She painted, or as she called it, "marked," in her small cabin. All of her work is of local scenes and happenings. "I sees it (the concept of the painting) in my sleep and I gets up and marks it." She continued to paint until just before her death in 1970. Her work is in the private collections of the Cane River country but is relatively unknown in the North.

As for "Washday": apparently everyone—even grandma—helped on washday at a time when hot water did not come from a pipe and when hands—not a machine—did the work.

COLOR KEY

☑ 1   Gray
☐ 2   Light Blue
◪ 3   Dark Brown
⊻ 4   Light Green
◼ 5   Black
   6   Gold
   7   Purple
   8   Dark Blue
   9   Dark Bronze
  10   Taupe
  11   White
⊡ 12   Cream
  13   Medium Blue
  14   Red
  15   Yellow
  16   Tweed   { 1 strand Medium Green / 1 strand Dark Green
  17   Tweed   { 1 strand Dark Brown / 1 strand Taupe
⊞   Tweed   { 1 strand Gold / 1 strand Bronze
☐   Tweed   { 1 strand Light Green / 1 strand Cream
☒   Medium Green

Washday

FINISHED SIZE:

12½″ × 13½″

MATERIALS:

13 mesh to the inch mono canvas. 3-ply Persian tapestry yarn in the colors indicated in the color key.

DIRECTIONS:

Bind the edges of the canvas with masking tape to prevent raveling. Separate the 3-ply yarn, using two strands together; following the chart and color key, work the needlepoint in the Diagonal Stitch. The tweed areas are worked with one strand of each color indicated. The wash on the lines, the fire, and the women's aprons, hats, and wash in the tubs are worked with all three strands in the Bargello stitches and colors shown in each area. The clothes pins are one long stitch with a large French Knot at the top.

Rose Kennedy's
Piano Bench Cover

Mary Hannon Fitzgerald, mother of Rose Kennedy, worked this piano bench cover in gros point when she was in her eighties. Her pattern is based on American wildflowers surrounded by the formal scallops of the Colonial period. Her work seems to have inspired her grandchildren and great-grandchildren, who have been known to make needlepoint slippers as presents.

   Mrs. Fitzgerald's needlepoint covers a bench in front of a grand piano—with sheet music from the twenties on the rack—in her daughter's home at Hyannisport.

COLOR KEY

- ☐ **1** White
- ☑ **2** Pink
- ☑ **3** Mauve
- ☑ **4** Deep Rose
- ☐ **5** Light Turquoise
- ☐ **6** Medium Turquoise
- ☒ **7** Dark Turquoise
- ☐ **8** Dark Blue
- **9** Medium Blue
- **10** Light Blue
- **11** Gray

Rose Kennedy's Piano Bench Cover

FINISHED SIZE:

13¾″ × 9¼″

MATERIALS:

14 mesh to the inch mono canvas. 3-ply Persian tapestry yarn in the colors specified in the color key.

DIRECTIONS:

Bind the edges of the canvas with masking tape to prevent raveling. Separate the strands of the 3-ply yarn, using two strands together. Starting at the upper right corner, work the design using the Diagonal Stitch. Follow the diagram and color key.

92

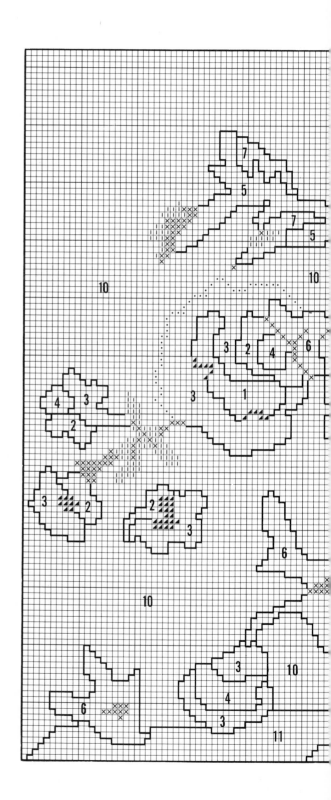

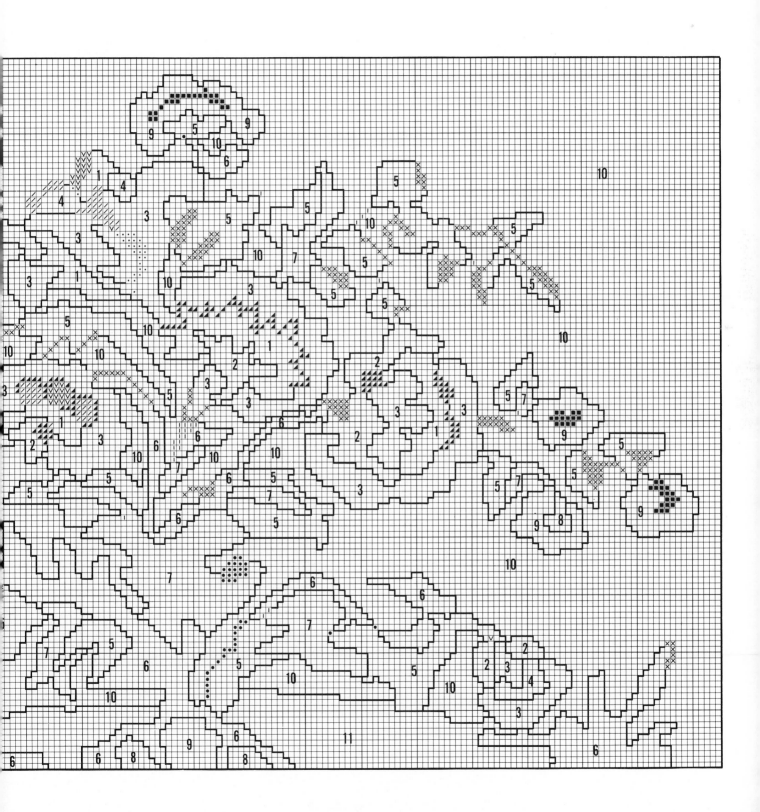

American Rose

This pattern is dedicated to Rose Fitzgerald Kennedy, who
wrote the Foreword to this book. The design was inspired
by the many cabbage rose designs popular from the
Colonial times to the present. Sketched on this page are
roses typical of the Civil War period.

◨ Dark Green
⊠ Olive Green
1 Dark Red
2 Dusty Rose
3 Pink
4 Pale Pink
5 Champagne
6 Gray

American Rose

FINISHED SIZE:

17⅜″ × 16″

MATERIALS:

10 mesh to the inch mono canvas. 3-ply Persian tapestry yarn in the colors indicated in the color key.

DIRECTIONS:

Bind the edges of the canvas with masking tape to prevent raveling. Work needlepoint in the Continental Stitch following the chart and color key.

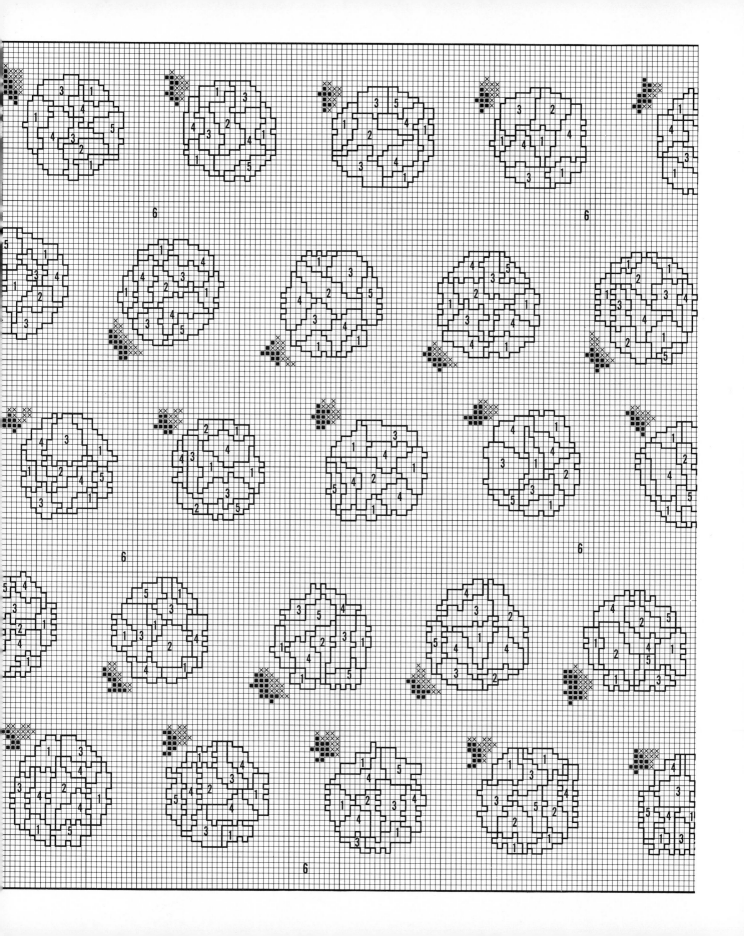

The Sailor's Farewell

The romantic scene of a sailor taking leave of his sweetheart was a popular theme of eighteenth-century Chinese export ware—porcelain made in China and decorated there expressly for export to the West. Enormous amounts of Chinese porcelain, along with silks and tea, came to America via Europe before the American Revolution. But following independence, American merchants began to trade directly with China for these prized goods.

This design is adapted from a tea bowl dating from the Colonial period and now displayed in the collection of the Museum of the American China Trade in Milton, Massachusetts.

COLOR KEY

- ◧ 1 Black
- ☐ 2 White
- ◩ 3 Brown
- ⊠ 4 Medium Green
- ☐ 5 Light Green
- ◿ 6 Chartreuse
- ⊡ 7 Yellow
- ☑ 8 Pink
- ◉ 9 Dusty Rose
- ⊡ 10 Gray
- ⑤ 11 Red
- ⊞   Blue
- ☐   Mint (background)

The Sailor's Farewell

FINISHED SIZE:

15½″ × 15¾″

MATERIALS:

12 mesh to the inch mono canvas. 3-ply Persian tapestry yarn in the colors indicated in the color key. One length of black embroidery floss.

DIRECTIONS:

Bind the edges of the canvas with masking tape to prevent raveling. Starting at the upper right corner, work the design using the Diagonal Stitch. Follow the diagram and color key. When the needlepoint is complete, use a single strand of black embroidery floss to outline the woman's arm and eyebrows in a simple straight stitch. If you prefer, these features can be drawn in with black acrylic paint.

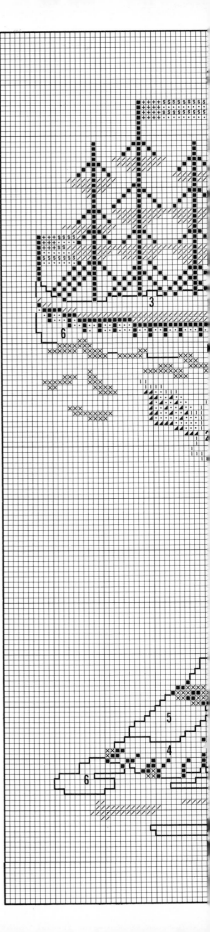

Molley Russell Sampler

This large sampler in the Smithsonian Institution is the only one bearing that famous date—1776—that I have found in the museums of this country. I have kept the pattern more or less unchanged for the needlepoint design, but reduced the text from the original poem of two four-line stanzas. Also, I deleted the word "gay," which originally came before the word "love," because of its newly ambiguous meaning.

In fact, the joy and peace that Molley Russell speaks of did not really exist in 1776. There would be five more years of fighting before peace arrived.

(Photograph courtesy of the Smithsonian Institution, Washington, D.C.)

COLOR KEY

- ⊡ **1** Dark Ochre
- ⊡ **2** Light Ochre
- ⊞ **3** Dark Teale
- ◩ Medium Teale
- **4** Light Teale
- ▢ Light Blue
- **5** Light Pink
- ⊙ Rose
- ⩔ Deep Rose
- ▣ Dark Brown
- ⊠ Medium Brown
- ▢ White (background)

Molley Russell Sampler

FINISHED SIZE:

17¾" × 13"

MATERIALS:

10 mesh to the inch Penelope canvas. Persian tapestry yarn in the colors indicated in the color key.

DIRECTIONS:

Bind the edges of the canvas with masking tape to prevent raveling. Work the needlepoint in the Continental Stitch, following the diagram and color key.

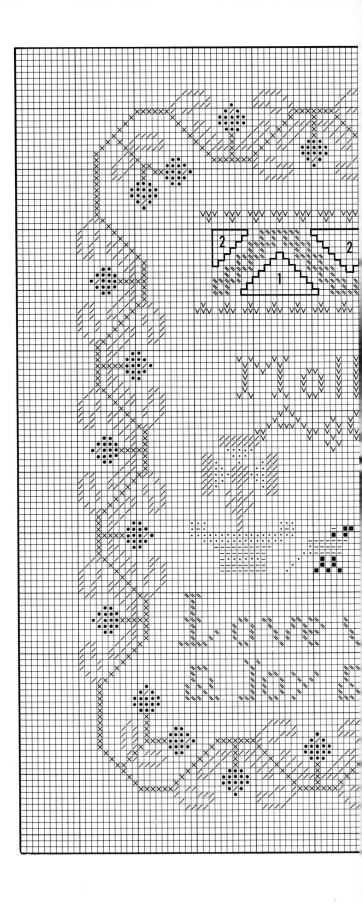

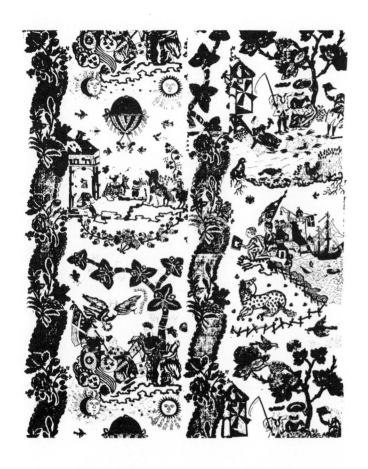

The Boston Tea Party

One of the most charming depictions of the Boston Tea Party is part of a four-scene toile designed and printed at Oberkampf's plant in Jouy between 1785 and 1790. *"L'Hommage de l'Amérique à la France"* was one of several fabrics produced with enthusiasm in honor of Lafayette and with one eye on sales to the Americans. It is now on display at the Museum of Printed Textiles in Mulhouse, France.

The print (from the nineteenth century) shows the patriots, disguised as Mohawks, dumping the tea from the ships into Boston Harbor, as empty chests bob in the water. After the Tea Party was over, John Adams was asked what he thought of it, and he answered, "The sublimity of it charms me."

1 White
2 Pale Blue
3 Medium Bright Blue
4 Light Slate Blue
5 Medium Slate Blue
6 Dark Slate Blue
7 Taupe
8 Deep Mustard
9 Medium Brown
10 Pale Brown
11 Deep Rust
12 Cinnamon
13 Salmon
14 Tan
15 Black

The Boston Tea Party

FINISHED SIZE:

13″ × 15″

MATERIALS:

Heavyweight natural-color linen. Crewel yarn in the colors specified in the color key. Transfer pencil or dressmaker's carbon.

DIRECTIONS:

Overcast the edges of the fabric or bind with masking tape to prevent raveling. Enlarge the pattern (see page 138) and transfer to the linen using transfer pencil or dressmaker's carbon. Use the Outline Stitch worked in black yarn for the heavier lines in the pattern. The fine lines in the sky are also worked in the Outline Stitch, in pale blue. The water is worked in a short straight stitch. Following the diagram and color key, work the remainder of the design in Satin Stitch, in the directions shown in the illustration.

108

United We Stand

Taken up by Americans during the Colonial and Revolutionary War period, this rallying cry goes back to Aesop's fable of *The Four Oxen and the Lion.* John Dickinson, known as the "Penman of the Revolution," used the lines in 1768 for the refrain of "The Liberty Song":

> Then join hand in hand, brave Americans all!
> By uniting we stand, by dividing we fall.

Some seventy years later, George Pope Morris—who also wrote "Woodman, Spare That Tree"—quoted the slogan in his popular poem "The Flag of Our Union."

I found the slogan worked into a beautiful handwoven coverlet from natural (undyed) and blue threads; the date 1840 is worked into the fabric.

COLOR KEY

⊠ Deep Blue
⊡ White

United We Stand

FINISHED SIZE:

17″ × 13¼″

MATERIALS:

14 mesh to the inch mono canvas. 3-ply Persian tapestry yarn in the colors specified in the color key.

DIRECTIONS:

The entire design is worked in two contrasting colors, using a variety of stitches. Work all needlepoint in the Half-cross Stitch, using only two strands at a time of the 3-ply yarn. For Bargello stitches, use all three strands. The outer border is worked in blue in the Bargello stitch indicated on the diagram. The lettering and scroll-work are done in needlepoint on a white Bargello background, as shown in the upper left corner of the diagram. The central pattern of white flowers, leaves, and crosses on a blue background is worked mainly in needlepoint. The centers of the flowers are white Bargello stitches; the very center of the large flower is in blue Bargello, and the centers of the smaller flowers are outlined with the blue straight stitches. Follow the diagram and the illustration to complete the design.

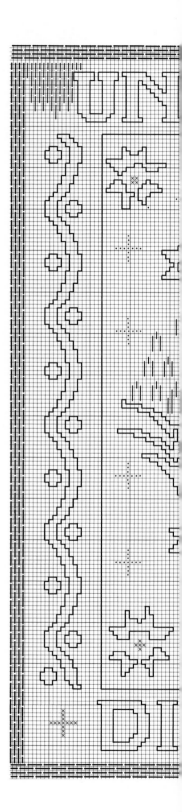

114

Clementine's Bouquet

Born in 1882 on a Louisiana plantation, Clementine Hunter worked variously at cotton picking, pecan harvesting, sewing, cooking, laundry, and whatever work presented itself.

Her flower painting arose from her love of flowers. She always had the best garden on the plantation and made sure everybody had a flower to wear on Sunday when the workers went to the Church of St. Mary's-on-the-Bayou.

COLOR KEY

▣	1	Purple
⊡	2	Kelly Green
◪	3	Light Green
⊠	4	Orange
⊞	5	Hot Pink
⧅	6	Lavender
	7	Brown
	8	Pale Pink
	9	Yellow
□	10	Off-White (background)

Clementine's Bouquet

FINISHED SIZE:

12″ × 12½″

MATERIALS:

12 mesh to the inch mono canvas. Persian tapestry yarn in the colors indicated in the color key.

DIRECTIONS:

Bind the edges of the canvas with masking tape to prevent raveling. Starting at the upper right corner, two canvas threads in, work the background, vase, and buds in the Diagonal Stitch. The flowers are worked with random straight stitches radiating from their centers. See the illustration for the color sequence in the three pink flowers. The dots in the center of the flowers are French Knots. Work the vase border and the mass of green leaves in the Bargello stitches indicated in the diagram. To work the border around the entire design, continue in the Bargello stitch marked in the lower right corner of the diagram, using the background color.

117

Mules in the Pasture

Until 1969, when she was 88, Clementine Hunter continued to paint her memories of plantation life in Louisiana. Her paintings—like "Pecan Harvesting," "Washday," "Wedding," "Sunday Church"—are gay and colorful. Even "Funeral" is bright with armloads of flowers and a vivid blue coffin.

"Mules in the Pasture" shows a workaday scene, with mules being driven out of the pecan orchard. The cowboys are clearly archetypal Early Hollywood, but the curtains at the top are just as clearly a simple stage—perhaps a memory of the small town theater in Nachitotches, Louisiana, where Clementine saw her first movies.

COLOR KEY

1	Dark Green		17	Light Blue
2	Medium Green		18	Pale Sky Blue
3	Kelly Green		19	Orange
4	Light Green		20	Gold
5	Olive Green		21	Red
6	Light Olive Green		22	Dark Rust
7	Deep Gray		23	Rust
8	Medium Gray		24	Deep Salmon
9	Light Gray		25	Light Salmon
10	Dark Brown		26	Pink
11	Medium Brown		27	Rose
12	Golden Brown		28	Deep Rose
13	Tan		29	Black
14	Beige		30	White
15	Dark Blue		31	Tweed { 1 stitch Mint / 1 stitch Light Green
16	Medium Blue			

Mules in the Pasture

FINISHED SIZE:

13″ × 13″

MATERIALS:

12 mesh to the inch mono canvas. Persian tapestry yarn in the colors indicated in the color key.

DIRECTIONS:

Bind the edges of the canvas with masking tape to prevent raveling. Work needlepoint in Diagonal Stitch, starting at the upper right corner. Follow the diagram and color key. The tweed in the lower background, marked color 31, is worked stitch by stitch in alternating colors to produce a checkerboard effect.

120

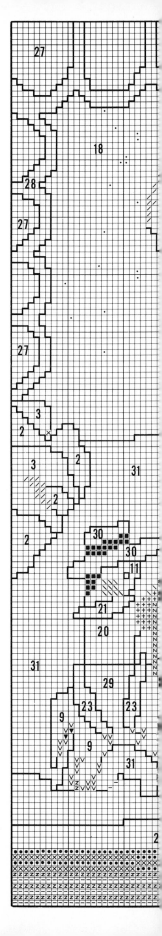

Eagle by William Schimmel.
Abby Aldrich Rockefeller Folk Art Collection

Eagles All Over

I looked at many, many carved and painted eagles, and the handcarved wooden ones were the most appealing in their simplicity. This design is from my sketch of the work by the famous Pennsylvania Dutch carver Wilhelm Schimmel. He was an itinerant sculptor who depended on his skill with the knife to see him through his countryside wanderings from one shop or tavern to the next. His fearless eagles stood guard over the Cumberland Valley for generations.

Ben Franklin wanted the national symbol to be the turkey because it is a completely American bird, and a peaceful one. But he and the other "doves" lost out to the "hawks" or, in this case, to the eagles.

123

COLOR KEY

⊠ 1 Brown
⊡ 2 White
⊡ 3 Gray
◪ Gold
⊞ Green
◼ Black
☐ Blue (background)

Eagles All Over

FINISHED SIZE:

14½″ × 15″

MATERIALS:

12 mesh to the inch mono canvas. 3-ply Persian tapestry yarn in the colors specified in the color key.

DIRECTIONS:

Bind the edges of the canvas with masking tape to prevent raveling. Beginning at the upper right corner, work the design using the Continental Stitch. All stars are in white; follow the diagram and color key to complete the pattern.

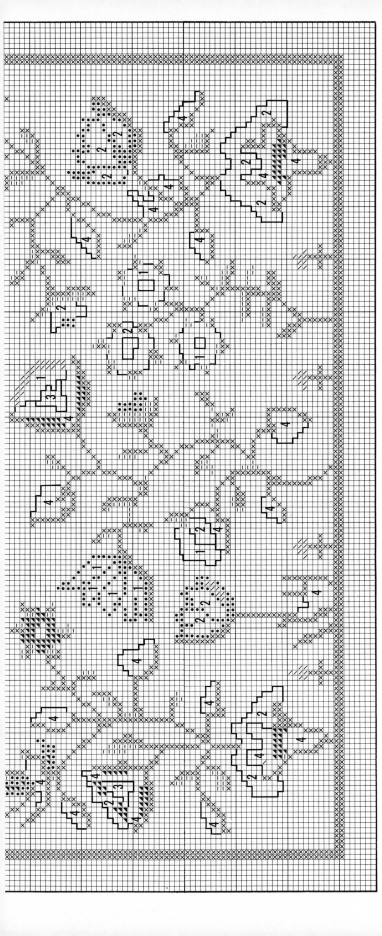

Alphabet Sampler

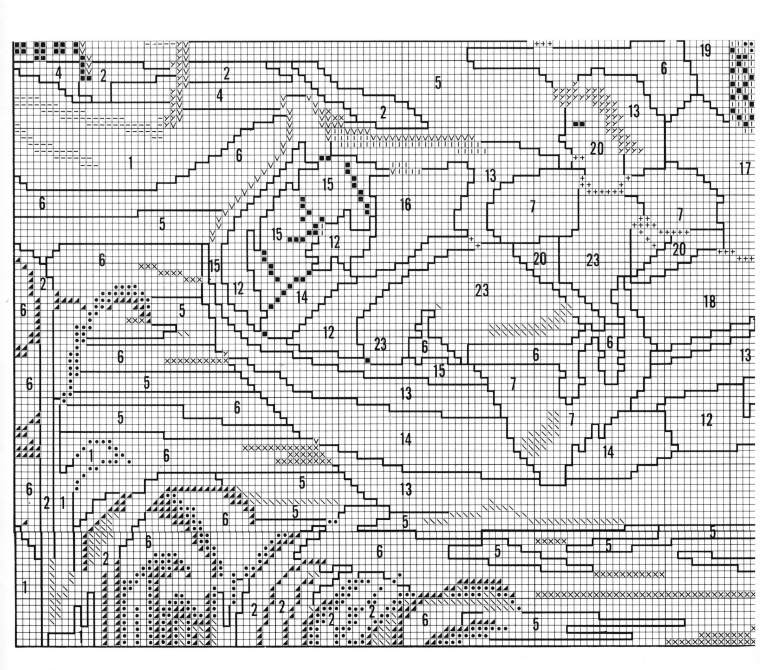

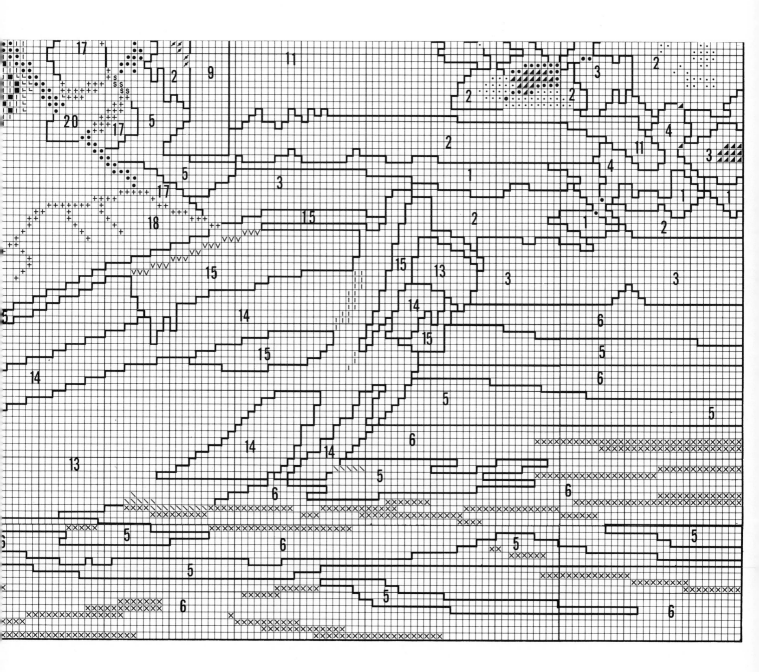

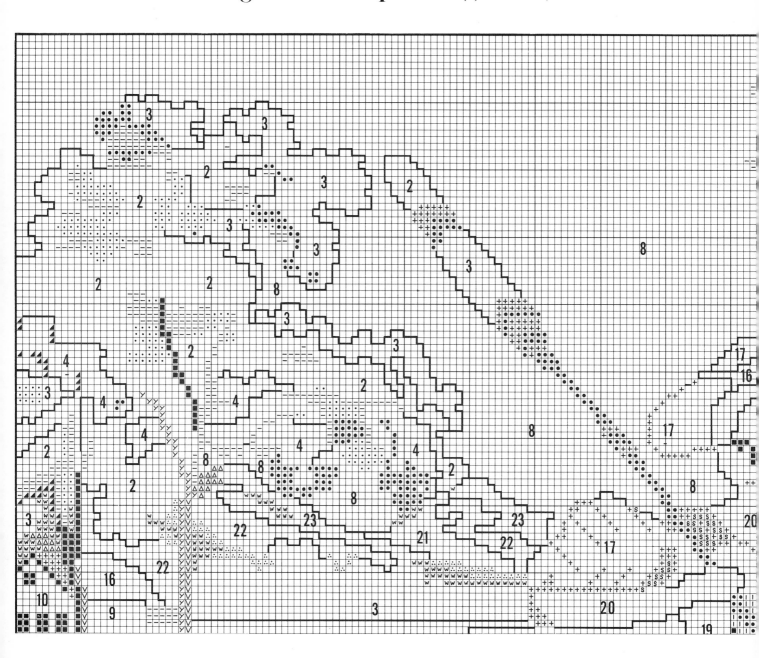

Benjamin Franklin Bouquet —upper left quarter

Benjamin Franklin Bouquet —lower half

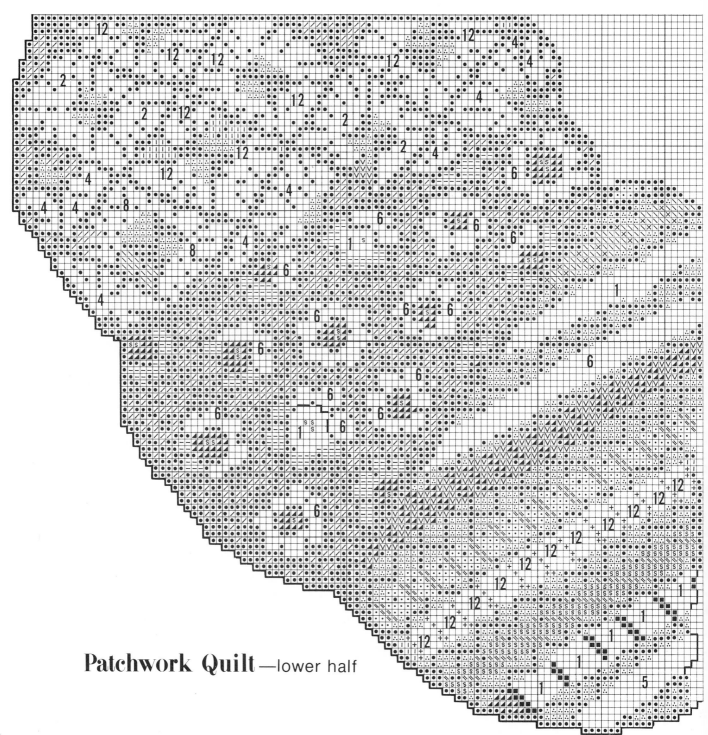

Patchwork Quilt —lower half

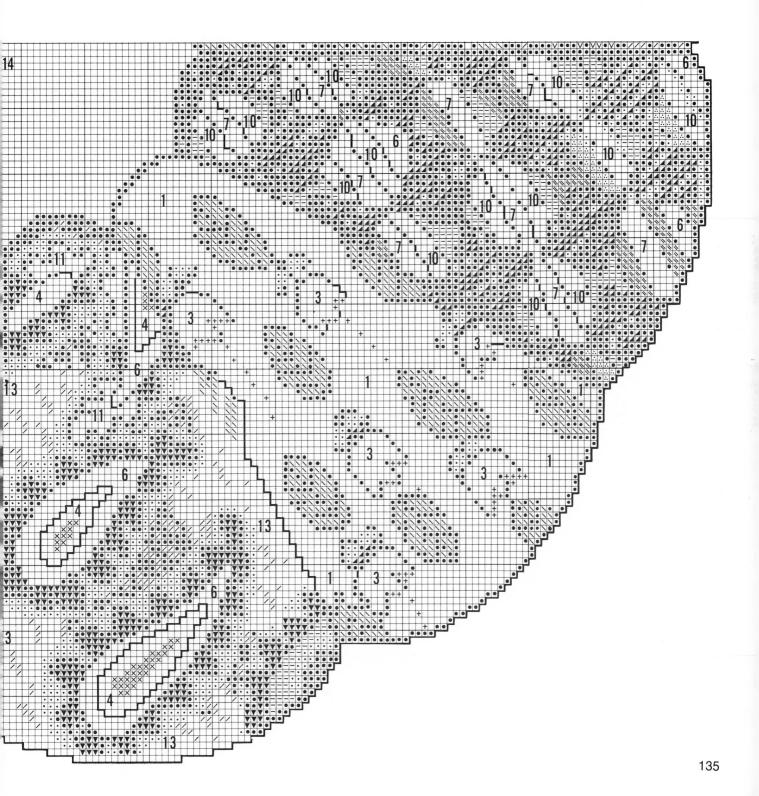

Patchwork Quilt —upper left quarter

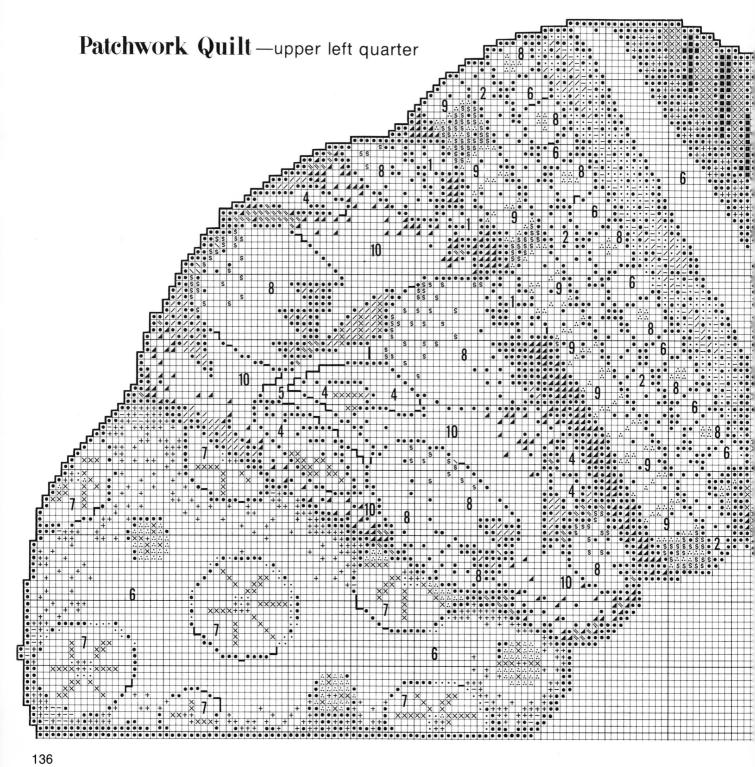

The Spirit of '76
—detail of area in upper right

TRANSFERRING PATTERNS

It's a simple matter to enlarge and transfer any of the patterns to your canvas or linen. You'll need tracing paper and transfer pencil (available in needlework departments) or dressmaker's carbon (available in fabric and notions departments).

First, mark off a sheet of plain tracing paper into squares of equal size—many people use 1-inch squares, others ½- or ¼-inch. Art supply stores also stock tracing paper marked with ¼-inch grids, and you may find this best. Place the tracing paper over the pattern and trace the design.

Now take a larger sheet of tracing paper and draw a rectangle indicating the desired finished size of your needlework. Mark this area off into the same number of squares used in your first tracing. Now redraw the design, square by square.

An even simpler method of enlarging is to make enlarged photostat of the pattern; a negative will do. Then redraw this on tracing paper.

The final step: transfer the enlarged pattern onto your canvas or linen using transfer pencil or dressmaker's carbon. For the first, retrace the pencil lines onto the *back* of the tracing paper with the transfer pencil. Center the tracing over the fabric, transfer-pencil markings toward the fabric, and press with a hot iron. (Directions are included with the transfer pencil, but that's the basic idea.) For smoother fabrics, dressmaker's carbon does a good job. Simply place the carbon paper between the tracing paper and the cloth, carbon side against the cloth, and go over the traced pattern lines firmly with a pencil or a semi-sharp point.

BLOCKING NEEDLEWORK

COTTON

Blocking is needed especially for wool needlepoint. The purpose is twofold: to square and straighten the worked canvas and to close up the stitches. This is accomplished by hot wetting the finished needlework after it has been properly pinned out and stretched.

In blocking pieces made with wool yarn, shrinkage plays a part (and when cotton yarn is used it is the principal action), but the process called "felting" plays the main role. The wool fiber can be visualized as a tube with scales like fish scales; the hot wetting causes the felting—the interlocking of these spiky scales, cementing the wool fibers together.

Everyone has his own procedure for blocking. I use a wooden drawing board with squares drawn on it, over which I put a sheet of clear vinyl. Then I tack the piece of needlework face down on the board using artists' aluminum push pins spaced an inch apart. I pin down one edge, lining it up with the guidelines drawn underneath, and then pull the opposite edge and pin it down along the nearest guideline. There is no need to pull hard—it is better to have the needlework merely flat, not tightly stretched. Then I pin the third side, keeping the needlework square, and finally, the fourth side. (If the piece is very distorted—out of square—the blocking must be done in two stages, because you can't correct it in one operation.)

I put a dish towel or a piece of muslin over the work and wet the towel with a clean kitchen sponge, using hot water, but not too hot to touch. The work must be thoroughly wet: a large cup of water is about right for a 14-inch square. Leave the needlework until it is bone dry, which usually takes two nights. And keep the cat away from it—cats sit on needlework and make a permanent dent!

If the work has a lot of "loft"—raised stitches, French knots, and so on—I pin it face up and hold a steam iron one-half inch above the work to wet it. The steaming eliminates pressure and preserves all the raised effects.

WOOL

BASIC STITCHES: NEEDLEPOINT

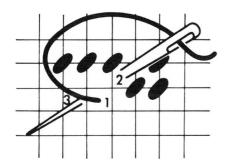

CONTINENTAL STITCH

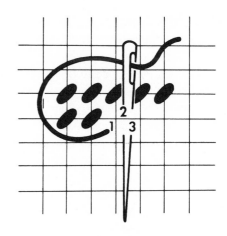

HALF-CROSS-STITCH

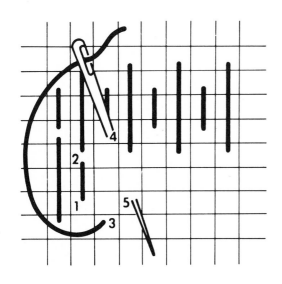

PARISIAN STITCH

140

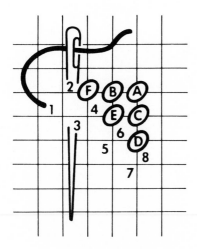

DIAGONAL STITCH—going down

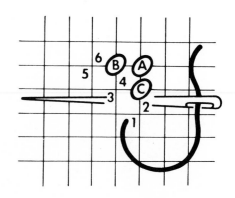

DIAGONAL STITCH—going up

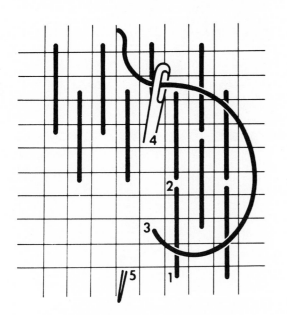

BRICK STITCH

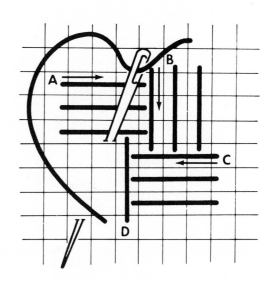

BASKET WEAVE BARGELLO

BASIC STITCHES: CREWEL

CROSS-STITCH

CHAIN STITCH

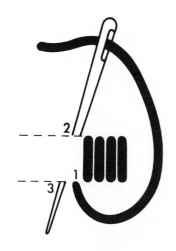

SATIN STITCH

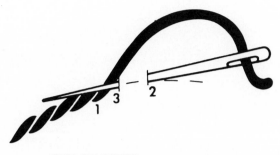

OUTLINE STITCH

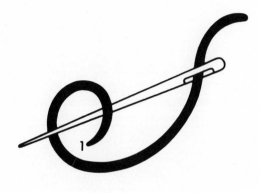

FRENCH KNOT A.

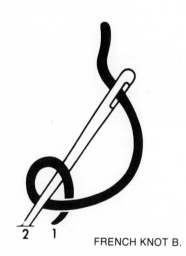

FRENCH KNOT B.

Home kits for the patterns illustrated on pages 14, 18, 22, 26, 30, 42, 54, 78, 90, and 122 have been prepared by the Crain Harmon Company, 799 Broadway, New York City 10003.